Live Life Out Loud

Living life out loud is scary, but not living life at all is much scarier.

Seeking purpose and striving to leave a legacy are innately human desires. Legacy can come in many forms - family, business ventures, art, music, literature, research and much more. Irrespective of what that ultimately looks like for you, finding and creating purpose in life requires the space to listen to your inner thoughts and desires. It takes the courage to pursue what you belive in and the discipline to work relentlessly towards big things.

This journal is dedicated to holding a space for honest reflection, building self awareness and exploring your passions, ideas and interests. You can work through its pages from cover to cover, or you can pick activities that speak to the topics that you most need to work through at this point in your life. I hope that in creating space to reflect and dream, you also create space for change and possibility in your life moving forward.

Laura x

Copyright © 2020 Laura Manescu

All rights reserved. No part of this book may be used or reproduced in any manner without the written permission of the author.

For information, contact:
Laura Manescu
www.linkedin.com/in/lauramanescu

ISBN 978-1-922357-03-8

Live Life Out Loud

"Respond to every call that excites your spirit."
— Rumi

Me, Myself And I

The relationship you have with yourself sets the bar that you hold up for every other relationship in your life. It is also a complex relationship, which takes time and dedication to improve. Self awareness is a crucial ingredient to being in a position to grow and become a better version of yourself every day.

The exercises in this section aim to create space for you to explore your own values, beliefs and intentions, in the hopes of building greater self awareness and supporting your personal growth.

"Life can only be understood backwards; but it must be lived forwards."
- Soren Kierkegaard

Who do you want to be?

What do you want to stand for?

The Quick Ten
Ten questions to get you reflecting.

1. Who has changed the direction of your life?

2. What quote do you live by?

3. What conversation will you always remember?

4. What was the last act of kindness you did for someone that you didn't know?

5. What is the best decision you've ever made?

The Quick Ten

6. When did you last feel inspired?

7. What is the best job you've ever had?

8. How did you meet your closest friend?

9. What book changed your thinking?

10. Which teacher has influenced you the most?

Reflecting On Change

Reflect on ten ways that you have changed, developed and grown in the past ten years.

1. _____

2. _____

3. _____

4. _____

5. _____

6. _____

7. _____

8. _____

9. _____

10. _____

Exploring Values

What matters to you?

_____

_____

_____

What beliefs in your life are unwavering?

_____

_____

_____

When have you been asked to do something that you strongly disagreed with?

_____

_____

_____

Exploring Values

What principles do you live by? Circle words that resonate and add your own.

Work ethic	Quality
Achievement	Heart
Kindness	Diversity
Creativity	Optimism
Challenge	Compassion
Adventure	Presence
Courage	Energy
Stability	Awareness
Certainty	Citizenship
Beauty	Peace
Patience	Love
Perfection	Learning
Growth	Humour
Change	Curiosity
Possibility	Fun

Exploring Values

Respect

Success

Equality

Accuracy

Focus

Decisiveness

Integrity

Justice

Trustworthiness

Boldness

Determination

Spirituality

Altruism

Open-mindedness

_____   _____

_____   _____

_____   _____

_____   _____

_____   _____

_____   _____

_____   _____

Exploring Values

Shortlist the ten values that most closely guide you in your life.

_____   _____

_____   _____

_____   _____

_____   _____

_____   _____

Now, pick the three values that most closely align with the way you live your life and what matters to you.

_____

_____

_____

Set this list aside for seven days and come back to complete the following reflection questions.

Exploring Values

How did these three values play out for you this week?

_____

_____

Are there other guiding factors that played out more regularly in your decisions, conflicts and relationships?

_____

_____

Finalise the three values that most closely guide you.

    _____

    _____

    _____

Come back to this exercise in three months' time and review whether these three values still resonate.

Priorities

Over the next 12-18 months, what areas of your life are your highest priorities?

Family	1.
Career	2.
Health	3.
Relationships	4.
Travel	5.
Finances	6.
_____	7.
_____	8.

"In today's rush, we all think too much, seek too much, want too much and forget about the joy of just being."
- Eckhart Tolle

Getting Centred

Get comfortable.

Start by connecting with your breathing. Take three deep breaths.

Picture yourself walking through a lush green rainforest. Follow the narrow, winding path through the ferns and trees. Notice the sound of birds in the trees above you and a rustle coming from a nearby shrub. There's a small stream flowing along the path and into the distance ahead of you.

Let yourself walk through this scene for a minute or two, continuing to breathe deeply.

If you get distracted by other thoughts, acknowledge them and gently bring your mind back to the rainforest.

As you walk through the rainforest, take in all of your senses. What can you smell? How hot or cold is it? Can you feel a breeze?

When you're ready, take three deep breaths and reconnect with the present.

Creating Mental Space

What activities or influences help you create mental space in your life?

Walking	Meditatation	Painting	Massages
Sport	Yoga	Craft	Reading
Podcasts	Movies	Drawing	Writing
Cup of tea	Baths	Dancing	Exploring
Travel	Music	Friends	Running

_____

_____

_____

What one incremental change can you make to create more mental space in your life?

_____

_____

Stop, breathe, listen.

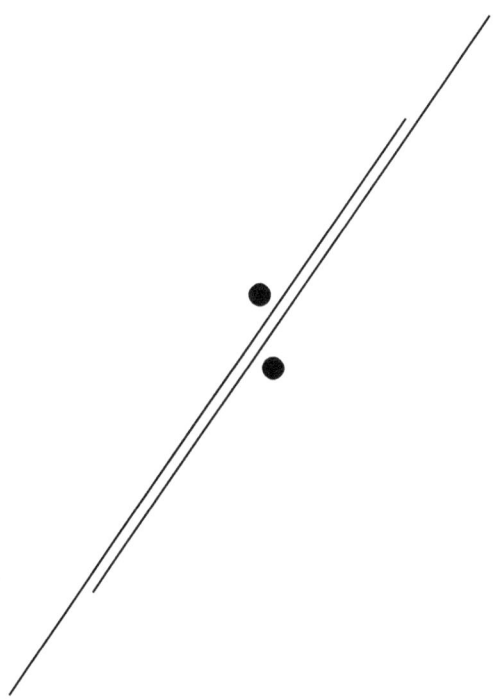

What comes to your mind first?

"If it doesn't challenge you,
it won't change you."
- Fred DeVito

Problem Solving

What challenge are you currently working through?

_____

_____

What is causing it?

_____

_____

What are three potential solutions?

_____

_____

_____

_____

Problem Solving

Which is most likely to get you the outcome you want?

_____

_____

_____

How will you make it happen?

_____

_____

_____

How did it go?

_____

_____

_____

Big Decisions

With an increasing range of choices, life presents you with many cross roads. Taking time for written reflection can help you process important decisions.

What are you trying to decide on?	
How might you benefit from doing it?	
How does it align with your priorities?	
If you don't do it, how will you feel in 3-5 years?	

Big Decisions

What is holding you back from going ahead?	
What can you do to overcome this?	
What other information do you need?	
Who else can support you with this decision?	
What is your gut telling you?	

Exploring Emotional Triggers

When are you at your worst?

_____

_____

_____

What triggers this state for you?

_____

_____

_____

How do you feel in this state? How do you react?

_____

_____

_____

Exploring Emotional Triggers

What can you do to reduce or limit exposure to your triggers?

_____

_____

_____

What helps you when you are in this state?

_____

_____

_____

Who in your life is good at managing this emotional state? How can they help you?

_____

_____

_____

Reflection Space

Reflection Space

Reflection Space

Reflection Space

"Your relationship with yourself sets the tone for every other relationship you have."
- Robert Holden

Relationships

Relationships influence the way that you think, behave, act, learn and grow. For this reason, it's crucial to invest in relationships consciously and to surround yourself with people who bring out the best in you.

You set the tone for other relationships in your life. Self-respect and taking the time to set clear boundaries is crucial to your long term happiness.

This section provides exercises that allow you to reflect on relationships in your life, work through the way you interact with challenging people and explore your needs within romantic relationships.

"You are the average of the five people you spend the most time with."
- Jim Rohn

Intentful Relationships

Many relationships are born out of convenience or history. Maintaining healthy connections requires reflection and tough decisions about which relationships allow you to be your best.

Who in your life fuels you?	Who in your life drains you?
_____	_____
_____	_____
_____	_____
_____	_____
_____	_____
_____	_____
_____	_____
_____	_____

Intentful Relationships

Who are the six closest people in your life and why do you value your relationship with them?

Name: _____

What they bring to your life: _____

_____

_____

Name: _____

What they bring to your life: _____

_____

_____

Name: _____

What they bring to your life: _____

_____

_____

Intentful Relationships

Name: _____

What they bring to your life: _____

_____

_____

Name: _____

What they bring to your life: _____

_____

_____

Name: _____

What they bring to your life: _____

_____

_____

Intentful Relationships

What do you notice about the relationships in your life that are fueling you?

_____

_____

_____

What do you notice about the relationships in your life that are draining you?

_____

_____

_____

What one change do you want to make based on your reflections?

_____

_____

_____

Who do you admire in your life?

Who can you be yourself around?

Thank Someone Important

Think about someone you are grateful for in your life. What do you need to thank them for that you've never had the chance to?

_____

_____

_____

_____

_____

_____

_____

_____

Now go and tell them!

"People are hard to hate close up. Move in."
- Brené Brown

Challenging Interactions

This exercise is designed to hold space for you to reflect on and work through a relationship that you find difficult.

What context do you know this person in?

_____

_____

How do you feel when you interact with them?

_____

_____

_____

What is it about them that you are finding difficult?

_____

_____

_____

Challenging Interactions

What are their values? What matters to them?

_____

_____

_____

What might be going on for them right now?

_____

_____

_____

How might they be perceiving you? Why?

_____

_____

_____

Challenging Interactions

What is outside your control about the situation?

_____

_____

_____

What are the benefits of improving this relationship?

_____

_____

_____

What can you do differently to improve the relationship?

_____

_____

_____

_____

Seek to ask: 'What is their story?',
not 'What is their problem?'

"True love cannot be found where it does not exist, nor can it be denied where it does."
- Torquato Tasso

Total Catch!

Loving yourself, being proud of your strengths and accepting your flaws are crucial to ensuring that you have a strong foundation for relationships in your life. Take the time to remind yourself 20 reasons that you are a total catch.

1.

2.

3.

4.

5.

6.

7.

8.

9.

10.

11.

12.

13.

14.

15.

16.

17.

18.

19.

20.

Relationship Mapping

Taking time to reflect on your relationship history holistically can give you perspective on what really matters. Map out your last five relationships and reflect on what worked, what didn't, how the relationship began, why it ended and what you learned from it.

❶ Current/recent relationship

❷ Past relationship

Relationship Mapping

3 Past relationship

4 Past relationship

5 Past relationship

Relationship Mapping

What common themes did you notice?

_____

_____

_____

When have you been at your best in a relationship?

_____

_____

_____

How can you apply these reflections in your current/ next relationship?

_____

_____

_____

The Love List

Being clear on both what you need and the deal breakers in a romantic relationship, is crucial to finding and maintaining an enduring connection.

Needs and non-negotiables	Deal breakers
_____	_____
_____	_____
_____	_____
_____	_____
_____	_____
_____	_____
_____	_____

Sense check your list with a close friend who can give you feedback, share things that they think that you need and challenge you on any unreasonable demands.

"Relationships don't last because of the good times; they last because the hard times were handled with care."

- Anmol Andore

Nurturing Your Relationship

Lasting love takes effort, care and work. Try these activities to help you nurture your relationship over time.

- [ ] Set a time each month to discuss the relationship with complete honesty and compassion.

- [ ] Commit to a weekly date night.

- [ ] Switch off technology one night a month and spend it together.

- [ ] Apologise for something you've never apologised for. Mean it.

- [ ] Keep compliment jars or lists for each other.

- [ ] Regularly set aside time to take turns speaking, with only questions permitted from the other.

- [ ] Try one new thing together every month.

- [ ] Do personal goal setting exercises together.

Honest Conversations

This exercise is designed to facilitate honest conversations, build understanding and to hold space for judgement-free discussion in your relationship.

What values do you both share?	
Where do your values differ?	
How can you minimise the impacts of this?	
What are both of your emotional triggers?	

Honest Conversations

How can you minimise the impacts of this?	
What do each of you need from your partner?	
How do each of you naturally express love?	
What do you need on a bad day?	
How do you like to be supported during difficult discussions?	

Reflection Space

Reflection Space

_____

_____

_____

_____

_____

_____

_____

_____

_____

_____

_____

_____

_____

Reflection Space

Reflection Space

"Find a group of people who challenge and inspire you, spend a lot of time with them, and it will change you forever."
- Amy Poehler

Career

With technology evolving the landscape across every industry, change is inevitable.

Increasing scale, complexity and innovation are rendering technical skills outdated more rapidly than ever before. This is also driving demand for a better balance between soft and technical skills in both traditionally technical and traditionally people-focused roles. Future proofing your career in this environment requires a greater emphasis on lifelong learning, an active effort to cross-skill and an eye for exploring innovation at the intesection of diverse and traditionally disparate fields. The pace of change also means that your 'dream job' may not exist in the market yet.

This section creates space to reflect on your skills, passions and needs, so that as the right opportunities come up, you can recognise them and are ready to pursue them.

"Our destiny is not written for us, it's written by us."
- Barack Obama

Career Satisfaction

Rank the factors below in order of impact on your career satisfaction in a job (1 most to 8 least important).

Interesting work	1.
Work-life balance	2.
Quality of leader	3.
Learning and development	4.
Exposure	5.
Pay	6.
Promotion opportunities	7.
Team culture	8.

Career Drivers

Taking a step back to reflect on what drives you at work, can help you more consciously seek those elements from future roles.

What do you really enjoy doing?	
What are you good at?	
What don't you enjoy doing?	
Who makes you want to come to work?	

Career Drivers

What would you change about your role?	
What has been your greatest career challenge?	
When have you discovered a new strength?	
When have you been happiest in your career?	
When do you feel most absorbed in your job?	

Career Mapping

Taking time to reflect on your career history can give you perspective on what really matters. Map out your last five roles and reflect on what you loved, what you didn't enjoy, how you fell into it and why you left.

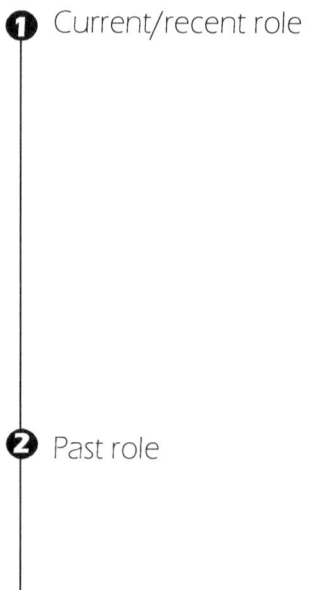

❶ Current/recent role

❷ Past role

Career Mapping

3 Past role

4 Past role

5 Past role

Career Mapping

What common themes did you notice?

_____

_____

_____

When in your career have you grown the most?

_____

_____

_____

How can you apply these reflections to your next career move?

_____

_____

_____

"Do the work that feeds your soul, not your ego."
- Jessica Walsh

Toxic Jobs

Eight signs it's time to leave your current job.

- [ ] Your job consistently triggers stress in your life.

- [ ] You don't believe in the company or vision.

- [ ] The skills you use in your role don't match your interests and passions.

- [ ] Your work significantly impacts your personal life, health, fitness, relationships and goals.

- [ ] Your value/potential is not recognised or used.

- [ ] You consistently watch the clock.

- [ ] You have learned a large proportion of what you set out to learn and have outgrown it.

- [ ] You've stopped thinking big or caring.

Looking Forward

In 18 months' time...

What do you want to have achieved?	
What skills do you want to have developed?	
What strengths do you want to be using daily?	

How is what you're doing today getting you closer to where you want to be tomorrow?

_____

_____

Evaluating Role Opportunities

When new opportunities come up, it can be easy to get caught up in the application process and the speed things are moving. Taking time to evaluate whether a new role is the right opportunity for you, will help guide you towards roles that you are truly passionate about.

Does this role use your strengths?

_____

_____

Does it align with your interests and passions?

_____

_____

Does the team culture suit your personality and needs?

_____

_____

Evaluating Role Opportunities

Does it enable the lifestyle you want?

_____

_____

How does it stack up against your career satisfaction drivers?

_____

_____

What key skills will you gain through the role? Are they your top priorities?

_____

_____

What future pathways and opportunities might it open?

_____

_____

Career Brainstorming

Put limitations on hold and jot down potential career paths that excite you...

Where can you
see yourself in
the future?

Building A Leadership Brand

True leadership means bringing the best out in the people around you and creating safe spaces for them to be seen and valued for who they are.

What kind of leader do you want to be?	
How do you want to make others feel?	
When do you lead at your best?	
What holds you back from your best?	

Reflection Space

Reflection Space

_____

_____

_____

_____

_____

_____

_____

_____

_____

_____

_____

_____

_____

_____

Reflection Space

Reflection Space

"A boss has the title, a leader has the people."
- Simon Sinek

Passions

There is an art to achieving balance in life: having a career that motivates you, surrounding yourself with people who bring out the best in you, and pursuing passions that fuel you. You have unique skills and strengths that can make a difference in the world outside of your career and your relationships.

This section creates space for you to dream big, identify what you care about most and set goals that inspire you. Take time to explore what you're passionate about and what else you can be doing to ignite the fire in your belly and leave a legacy that you're proud of.

"If not us, then who? If not now, then when?"
- John E. Lewis

What is your why?

When do you get to live your why?

Identifying Passion Spaces

What activities make you feel so absorbed that you lose track of time?

_____

_____

_____

What gets you really excited?

_____

_____

_____

What topics do you find yourself regularly bringing up with people and sharing your perspective on?

_____

_____

_____

Identifying Passion Spaces

What do you believe needs to change in the world to make it a better place?

_____

_____

_____

Who lives a life that you aspire to? What about them or their life inspires you?

_____

_____

_____

What did you love to do as a child?

_____

_____

_____

Identifying Passion Spaces

What would you do with your time if you had enough money not to work out of financial necessity?

_____

_____

_____

Who lights the fire in you and inspires you to something bigger than yourself?

_____

_____

_____

What would you do if you knew you couldn't fail?

_____

_____

_____

If you were promised your ideal life, what would it look like?

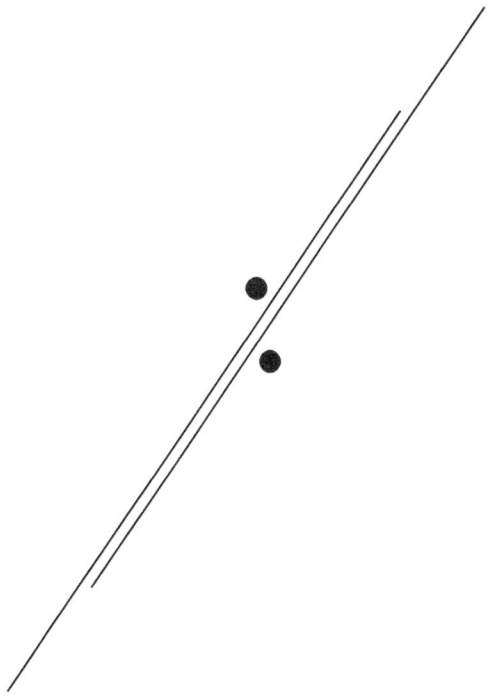

If today was your last day, what would you do with it?

"Set a goal that commands your thoughts, liberates your energy and inspires your hopes."
- Andrew Carnegie

Goal Setting

Setting goals that truly motivate you will help you persevere through challenges along the way.

Goal one

What do you want to achieve? By when?	
How will you know that you've been successful?	
What challenges might you face along the way?	
Who can help you get there?	

Goal Setting

Goal two

What do you want to achieve? By when?	
How will you know that you've been successful?	
What challenges might you face along the way?	
Who can help you get there?	

Goal Setting

Goal three

What do you want to achieve? By when?	
How will you know that you've been successful?	
What challenges might you face along the way?	
Who can help you get there?	

"Everything you want is on the other side of fear."
- Jack Canfield

Do something that scares you today!

Tackling Fear

What decision is scaring you at the moment?

_____

_____

_____

What is the worst thing that could happen?

_____

_____

_____

What can you do to prevent this happening?

_____

_____

_____

Tackling Fear

What can you do if the worst does happen?

_____

_____

_____

Who can help you if the worst does happen?

_____

_____

_____

What do you stand to gain from taking a chance?

_____

_____

_____

Embracing Fear

At times your passions may sit on the other side of your fears. Rewire your habits by challenging yourself to face your fears for 30 days.

Today I...

Day 1:

Day 2:

Day 3:

Day 4:

Day 5:

Day 6:

Day 7:

Day 8:

Day 9:

Day 10:

Day 11:

Embracing Fear

Day 12:

Day 13:

Day 14:

Day 15:

Day 16:

Day 17:

Day 18:

Day 19:

Day 20:

Day 21:

Day 22:

Day 23:

Day 24:

Day 25:

Embracing Fear

Day 26:

Day 27:

Day 28:

Day 29:

Day 30:

What did you notice during this exercise?

_____

_____

_____

What will you do differently going forward?

_____

_____

_____

"You can never cross the ocean until you have the courage to lose sight of the shore."
- Christopher Columbus

Wanderlust

Travel brings new perspectives, connections, memories, ways of thinking and lessons. Taking time to reflect on travel helps keep those perspectives front of mind.

What sight took your breath away?	
Who changed your life during your travels?	
What is your favourite travel memory?	
What have you learned while travelling?	

Travel Bucket List

What destinations are top of your list?

Adventure
destinations

Relaxing
destinations

Cultural
destinations

Beautiful
destinations

"You cannot have a positive life and a negative mind."
- Joyce Meyer

Protecting Energy

Your energy is impacted every day by the people you spend time with, the food you eat, the amount you sleep, the activities you do and everything you surround yourself with.

What builds you up?	What brings you down?
_____	_____
_____	_____
_____	_____
_____	_____
_____	_____
_____	_____

Commitment to start doing weekly:

Commitment to stop doing:

Happiness Hits

Seven actions for an instant pick-me-up.

- [ ] Send a thank you message to someone who has changed your life for the better.

- [ ] Watch your favourite childhood movie.

- [ ] Eat your favourite meal over a good book.

- [ ] Find a place with a nice view and watch the sunset.

- [ ] Ask a friend to go for a coffee and walk with you, out of the blue.

- [ ] Try something new: a restaurant, a suburb you haven't visited before, a volunteering activity.

- [ ] Get outside and do a workout.

Reflection Space

Reflection Space

Reflection Space

Reflection Space

Reflection Space

"Today I will do what others won't, so tomorrow I can do what others can't."
- Jerry Rice

www.ingramcontent.com/pod-product-compliance
Lightning Source LLC
Chambersburg PA
CBHW040416100526
44588CB00022B/2846